IMAGES OF ENGLAND

HARTLEPOOL
1946–1997

DOUGLAS R.P. FERRIDAY

The
History
Press

First published 1997

Reprinted 1999, 2004, 2008, 2012

Copyright © Douglas R.P. Ferriday, 2008

The History Press
The Mill, Brimscombe Port,
Stroud, Gloucestershire, GL5 2QG
www.thehistorypress.co.uk

ISBN 978 0 7524 0795 1

Typesetting and origination by
Tempus Publishing.
Printed and bound in England.

Storage of pit props on the dock area ready for transporting to the Durham coalfields, 1963.

IMAGES OF ENGLAND

HARTLEPOOL
1946–1997

The Croft Gardens in 1950 looking very smart and tidy. Little has changed except that now these are mature trees and bulbs in the gardens.

Contents

Acknowledgements

The author, who supplied a vast number of his own photographs, would like to thank all the following people who also loaned photographs for this book. Including; Marjorie and Ron Richardson, Ron Blair, John Robson, Alison Corbett, Gus Thompson, Raymond and Peter Stonehouse, J. Horn, Dennis Wompra.

The author would also like to thank
Hartlepool Mail, Northern Echo

Bibliography

A *Hartlepools Chronology*, J.M. Ward
Hartlepool Town Guides, 1960s/1970s
West Hartlepool Local Government Exhibition, 1946
Hartlepool Charter Celebrations, 1951
West Hartlepool Rugby Football Club, 1981
British Transport Docks
The Book of Hartlepool, D.R.P. Ferriday

An outing from the Blacksmiths Arms, Stanton, c. 1950.

Fifty Years of Change

At the end of the Second World War the Hartlepools prepared for a 'land fit for heroes', unaware of the many changes which were to take place in the forthcoming fifty years. Great rebuilding programmes were commenced, especially house building in the late 1940s up into the 1970s. The period during the 1960s was the most productive and yet at the same time was a most destructive one for the Hartlepools. Considerable demolition was carried out and many 'quick fix' structures erected. This was a decade which has a great deal to answer for architecturally, not only in Hartlepool but throughout the country. A time of change indeed!

Fortunately a rethink in the 1980s and '90s witnessed a re-emergence of traditional quality buildings with flair and imagination, the consequences of which can be seen in current housing, commercial and leisure complexes. Perhaps the 1990s has had the greatest visual impact on Hartlepool especially in the town centre and Marina areas, together with refurbishment of 'old' housing stock. This augers well for the future of a town which already has a long and proud history.

Just some of the many events to effect Hartlepool since the end of the Second World War include:

In 1946 Mr Max Lock was appointed to produce an overall planning scheme for the town which was completed in 1948. Although it was not acted upon until the middle of the 1960s when a greatly amended scheme was introduced. Foggy Furze Branch library was named in 1947. A fire at Seaton Timber storage yard caused considerable damage to stored timber.

During the 1950s the Seaton Carew swimming baths were re-opened after use as wartime barracks. The decade also saw the 'mothball' fleet arrive at the docks. The last trolley bus made its final journey from West Hartlepool to Hartlepool in 1953. The BKS air service ran its inauguration flight in May 1953 from West Hartlepool to London Northolt using Douglas Dakota DC3 planes. Cameron's Strongarm Beer was introduced in 1955.

Brierton Hill Technical School for girls was opened in 1961. Possibly the greatest trauma ever to hit the Hartlepool's was the shock closure of Wm Gray's shipyard and central marine engine works in 1962 which at the time employed 2,000 people, although this figure had been as high as 5,000 at one time. The closure was to have far reaching effects upon the twin towns for generations to come. In 1964 Edward Leadbitter was elected as Member of Parliament. Compulsory Purchase Orders were issued for Lynn Street in preparation for the new shopping centre. On 1 April 1967 (April Fools' Day) Hartlepool amalgamated with West Hartlepool and on the 7 April Councillor Fred Jacques was installed as the first Mayor of the new town. An era ended with the filling in of Swainson Dock early in 1968. Work began on the new General Hospital in April 1969 and the College of Further Education was officially opened on 26 April the same year. The final Town Show was held in Ward Jackson Park in August 1969 and September saw the opening of the new College of Art in Church Square. In 1969 the population was assessed at 100,000. In the 1960s regular dances were held in the Town Hall, Borough Hall and the Queens Rink Ballroom as well as in the two leading hotels, the Grand and the Staincliffe. There were 47 churches, 10 banks and 3 cinemas – the ABC (Forum), the Essoldo (Regal) and the Odeon.

The Windsor Restaurant was officially opened in July 1970 and the Annual Show was moved to Grayfields in the same year. In 1972 the Queens Rink Ballroom was demolished and Mill House Swimming Baths opened in March. Throston Bridge was demolished and the Wesley chapel closed, as did Christ Church in 1973. In September 1974 the Empire Theatre was pulled down. The first Open Market opened in March 1976. Queen Elizabeth II opened the Civic Centre and named *The Scout* lifeboat after touring the shopping centre in July 1977. In December 1977 the last steel was produced at the steelworks. HMS *Warrior* arrived at the Coal Dock for a full restoration in 1979. Henry Smith School and Suttons Fish Curing House were demolished in 1982. In 1983 pensioners free bus passes were introduced and the Nuclear Power Station came into operation. Hartlepool Police Station opened in April 1984 as did the Fire Brigade HQ in the former steelworks offices.

During the eventful 1980s and 1990s many notable major projects took place including; Hartlepool Marina, the Historic Quay, the Museum of Hartlepool, Christ Church Art Gallery, the Mail Office and Benefits Agency, Central Library, Jackson's Landing Factory Shopping, Tees Bay Retail Park, the Shopping Centre, Wesley chapel, Victory Square, the Old Municipal Buildings, the Town Hall Theatre, Church Street, Hartlepool United Victoria Park, restoration of older housing, the *Wingield Castle* Paddle Steamer, HMS *Trincomalee* and there are further schemes in the pipeline. In recent years over £400 million has been invested in the town by government and private funding.

Much has changed over the years, sometimes for the better and sometimes not, but overall the town has responded sensibly and well to change with people leading and needing different lives to our forebears. The townsfolk can be occasionally critical of their own town but defend it defiantly and vehemently when others, perhaps less well informed, attempt to run it down often without having visited the town.

One

The Town

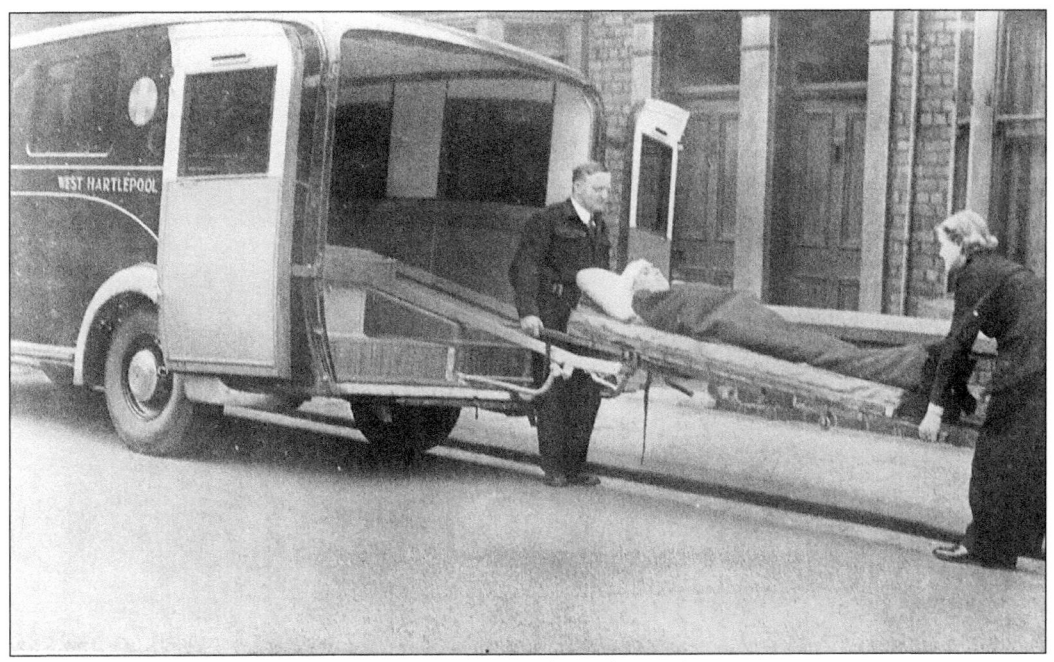

Corporation Free Ambulance Service, West Hartlepool, 1946.

An aerial view of the Dyke House area including Dyke House School at the centre in 1946. To the rear is Price's Tailors factory and the Powlett Road Gas Works is visible.

An aerial view of Hartlepool Headland, 1948. The Coal Staithes and New Fish Quay are visible at the top, with St Hilda's church in the centre and Hartlepool Hospital to the right.

The colourful Croft Gardens with St Hilda's church in the background, c. 1950. The light coloured house in front of St Hilda's church tower was the home of the soldier and historian Sir Cuthbert Sharp, Bt.

The War Memorial, Cliff Terrace and the Lighthouse, 1950. Nearby is the site of the infamous German naval bombardment of 1914 where the first British soldier was killed on home soil in the First World War.

Church Street from Christ Church tower looking east, c. 1950. Birks Cafe and Hotel is at the corner of Station Approach leading off from the left. Trolley Buses would traverse the wide expanse of this popular street.

CHURCH STREET, WEST HARTLEPOOL.

H.9192

Upper Church Street, West Hartlepool in 1950. To the left, where the traffic is stationary, a policeman directing traffic would stand in all weathers on a plinth on point duty.

A postcard from around 1950, although some of the photographs are obviously pre-war.

A good luck postcard still available in the shops in the 1940s and '50s although of pre-war vintage.

A snow scene in Lynn Street during the 1950s showing a trolley bus, the Star Hotel and Smarts the tailor.

The Croft Gardens and the harbour entrance from St Hilda's church tower, 1951.

The statue of Ralph Ward Jackson in the process of re-installation in Church Square by Clarence Erection Co. after being deposed by a passing bus in 1957.

Greatham Hospital of God, south of Hartlepool, c. 1960. It was founded after 1264 by Bishop Stickel of Durham for the welfare of retired elderly clergy.

The town Christmas tree being erected in the grounds of Wesley chapel ready for the Christmas carol singing and service, c. 1960.

The interior of Christ Church, Church Square in 1961. The splendid organ pipes can be seen on the left. This deconsecrated building now houses Hartlepool Art Gallery.

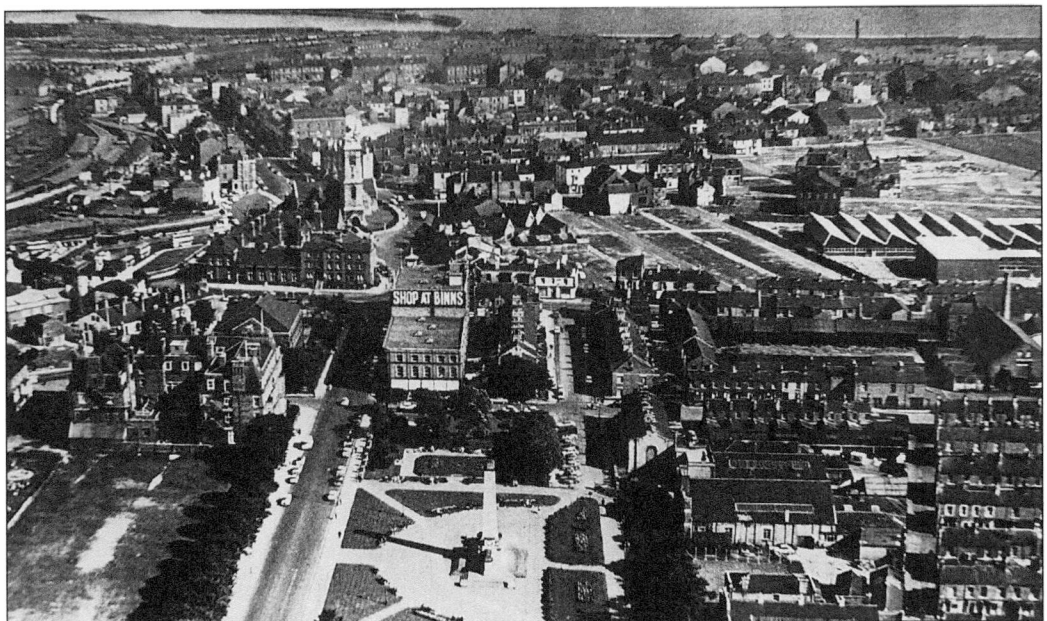

An impressive view of West Hartlepool town centre showing Binns in the centre. To the right of the War Memorial is the Armoury and TA Centre. The newly built College of Further Education is clearly visible, centre, right. At the bottom left is the Bull Field later used to build the Civic Centre. Most of the housing to the right and in the background was cleared ready for the redevelopment that included Middleton Grange shopping centre.

The 'Big Wesley' and Binns department store in Victoria Road, 1964. The squared-off top of Binns was removed in 1996 and the facade of the church restored for leisure use and shopping in 1997.

Swainson Street in November 1964 with the tower of the now-demolished Park Road Presbyterian church prominent in the distance. Some of the houses had small front gardens providing a 'green' aspect to what was a town centre environment. Note the area free from yellow lines!

Heslop & Hall, Andrew Street, the Co-op Central stores in Stockton Street, and the rear of Musgrave Street viewed from the roof of the College of Further Education during its construction in 1965.

Throston Bridge, Hartlepool, December 1965. The posters advertise Envoy Cigarettes at 4s 3d per packet, Cossack whiskey and Palethorpes sausages.

Victoria Road prior to the building of Middleton Grange shopping centre and the Civic Centre, 1966.

The old Railway Station in Mainsforth Terrace, 1966. The upper floor curved area to the left was the Board Room.

The platform within the Mainsforth Terrace Station in 1966 when it was used as a goods station.

Thornton Street during demolition in preparation for the new Middleton Grange shopping centre, 1966.

A fine view of Church Street looking east from the top of Christ Church tower, 1966.

A picture of tranquillity in Elwick village during May 1966, which has changed little over the years.

The Front, Seaton Carew, September 1966. There was bingo daily in the old chapel building.

Cottages on the Front at Seaton Carew with the Seaton Hotel on the right in September 1966. These were the halcyon days of no parking restrictions.

An aerial view of Seaton Carew North, September 1966. The Staincliffe Hotel is the fine looking building in the foreground, complete with tennis courts and kitchen garden.

Old Cemetery Road, Hartlepool, October 1966. They are having a natter about the 'old days' perhaps!

The rear of the Market Buildings in Lynn Street showing the interesting and unusual chimney in the yard. This yard was used as winter quarters by travelling showmen and their families.

Stockton Street, November 1966. The Picture House, later the Gaumont and latterly a Bingo Hall, is on the left and Foster & Armstrong Anchor Mills on the right.

The central area of Hartlepool in 1967. Many new developments are visible although the old town is yet to be cleared.

York Road and Park Road corner with Ewart Parsons petrol filling station and car showrooms, 1967. The site is currently occupied by Titan House. In the background is St George's church hall, a venue for numerous functions.

Henry Smith School and St Hilda's Hospital in the 1960s. The original school building is on the right. The centre and left sections were added over the years to accommodate more pupils. At the top right is the Morrison Hall.

Baltic Street, Hartlepool ready for demolition in May 1968.

An aerial view of Hartlepool Headland, Northgate, 1968. Just behind the two white buildings stood Hartlepool Railway Station. On the opposite side is the North Eastern Co-operative store and towards the sea Galley's Field School is just visible. Near to the quayside several marine and engineering companies provided services. Two engine sheds are also located to the right and formed part of the railway station complex.

Stockton Street at the corner of Musgrave Street and Park Road in the 1960s. Little survives today apart from the Binns' clock in the distance which is now part of Wilkinsons store. The dark building to the left is the Salvation Army citadel and Pierce the optician on the right provided a splendid clock.

Wards Terrace, West Hartlepool, October 1966.

King Street, Hartlepool, December 1969.

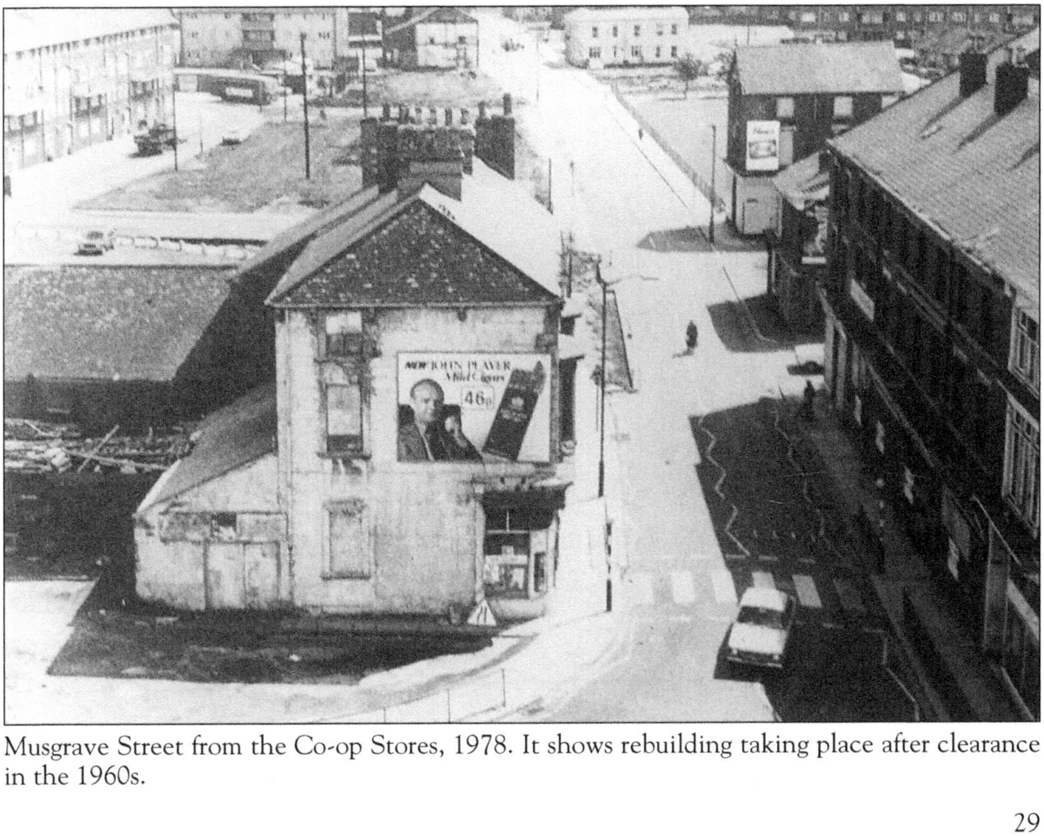

Musgrave Street from the Co-op Stores, 1978. It shows rebuilding taking place after clearance in the 1960s.

A 1970 advertisement for the Grand Hotel, Swainson Street. It was then owned by British Transport Hotels, and was one of 33 throughout the country.

Here's where you will dine
English and Continental cuisine backed up by superlative wines.

The Cocktail Bar
— where all the leading figures in Hartlepool meet their friends.

...and this is the magnificent Ballroom, set for a banquet
For all social occasions and business conventions.

Grand Hotel, Hartlepool. Tel: Hartlepool 66345

BTH 33 hotels that care about comfort.

Notification of the Driving Test in September 1959.

An aerial view of Hartlepool shopping centre, Civic Centre, and War Memorial in 1987.

Victory Square and Middleton Grange shopping centre in 1987.

Hartlepool Civic Centre, Victoria Road in 1987.

A view from the roof of the College of Further Education showing Stockton Street and the Middleton Grange shopping centre.

Two

The Best Years ...

Grantully Day Nursery, Westbourne Road, 1946. The children are enjoying the open air, supervised by numerous members of staff. This well used nursery was one of the earliest to be set up in the town after the war.

Park Road Modern School sports group in the 1950s. In the centre, with the shield, is Thomas Brown jnr.

Elwick Road Girls Secondary Modern School, prize winners presentation, 1959.

Scholarship winners from Newburn School being presented to the Mayor and Mayoress in 1955. Left to right: Ronald Blair, Jeffrey Davies, David Easton, Maureen Tull, Dorothy Rayner and headmaster, Mr Jolly.

Elwick Road Secondary Modern School Juniors, 1959. At least the teacher looks happy!

Brierton School group, 1958/59.

Galley's Field School near to the Town Moor in the 1960s. Galley's Court Sheltered Housing now occupies the site.

The combined choir of primary school children at the first concert to be conducted by Peter J. Haughton in the Borough Hall after months of hard preparation work in 1968.

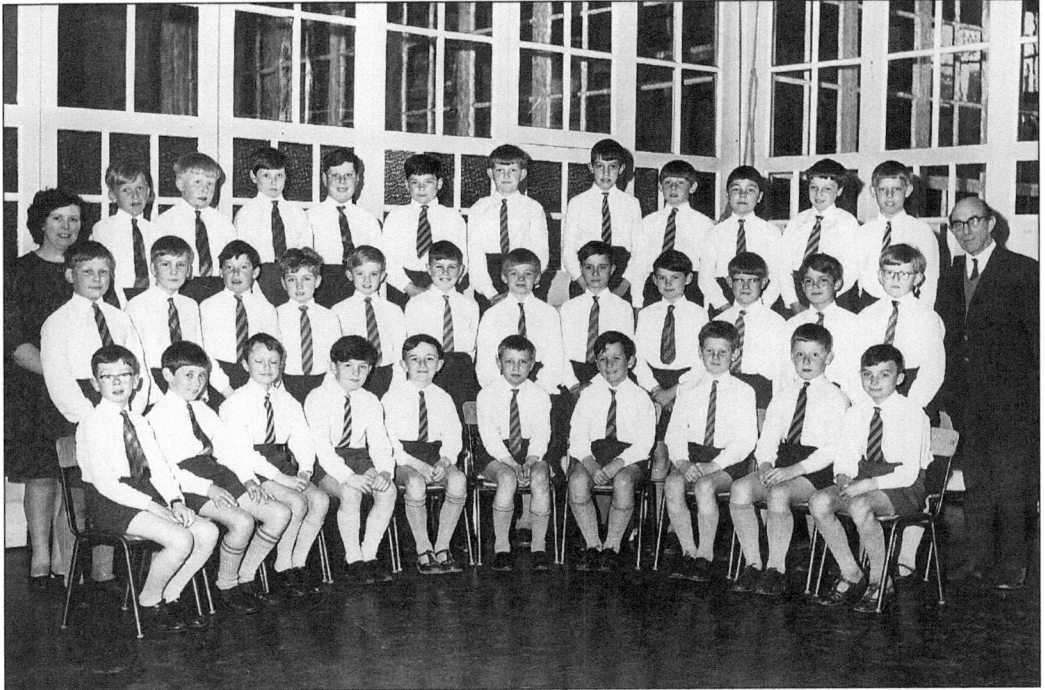

Elwick Road Junior Boys Choir, 1968. The conductor was Marjorie D. Richardson and the pianist George Davison. This popular choir gave many concerts entertaining the elderly and other groups.

HARTLEPOOL EDUCATION COMMITTEE

Chief Education Officer:

A. D. JACKSON, M.A.

Physical Education Organiser:

D. H. WILLIAMS

David Brown 4B is hereby awarded

the *Credit* certificate for proficiency

in the following:—

I	BREAST STROKE	5	DIVING
2	FRONT CRAWL	6	DISTANCE SWIMMING
3	BACK CRAWL	7	PERSONAL SURVIVAL
4	BUTTERFLY	8	LIFE SAVING

R Sands

1968

Senior Swimming Teacher

David Brown's distance swimming certificate, 1968.

Business Studies Department students at the College of Further Education, 1969.

A classroom in Barnard Grove County Infant School, February 1972.

Throston County Primary School, 1973, showing the cloakroom/activity area.

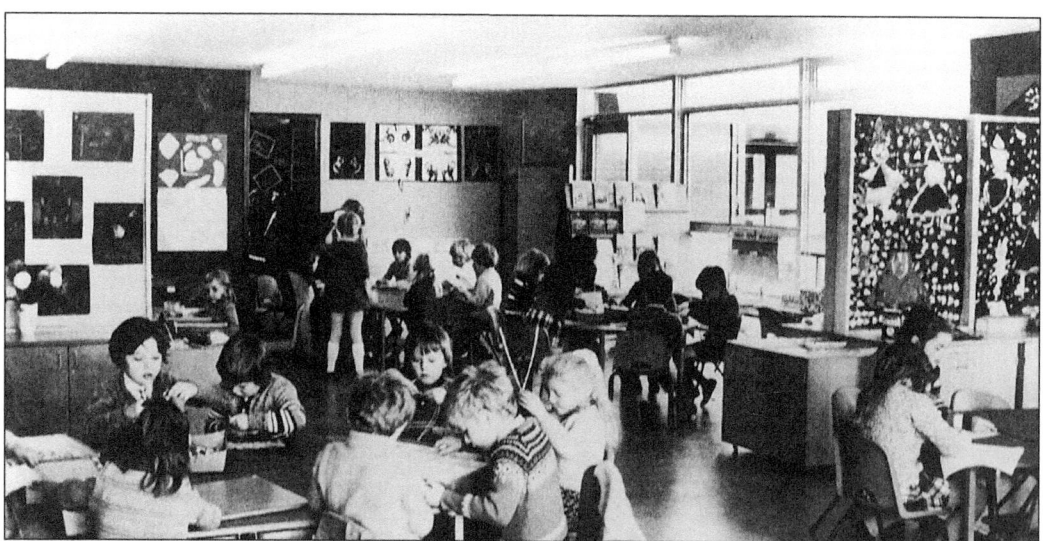

High Tunstall County Comprehensive School, 1974. This was the typing room in block 'C'.

Clavering County Primary School, practical area, 1974.

Three

Shopping Delights

A splendid Christmas window display in Walter Willsons ('Smiling Service'), Stockton Road near Foggy Furze, December 1965. Some of the items on offer are; shandy 11d, shortbread 1s 6d, puddings 2s 4d, mincemeat 1s 6d, icing sugar 1s, tall tins of John West salmon 6s 11d.

John's cycle shop in Stockton Road, near to St Aidan's in the 1950s. The shop later changed to selling televisions and radios. John Taylor, the proprietor, is standing in the doorway.

A busy Lynn Street on a Saturday afternoon in the 1950s. All the buildings shown are now demolished. Robinsons is in the distance and the Chain Lending Library is on the right. Only three cars are on this well used and popular street. The regular 'Saturday shopping quadrangle' was from Church Street, go down Lynn Street to Robinsons then along Musgrave Street to the Central Stores and along Stockton Street to Binns and back along Church Street via Church Square. Or you could travel the reverse route if the mood directed.

Lynn Street looking north at the junction with Musgrave Street, c. 1950.

The interior of Duncans provision shop in York Road, February 1966. Some of the provisions available and displayed on the counter are; pink salmon 1s 6d, kemps devonet 1s a packet and HP biscuits 1s (save 6d).

Vicarage Gardens, November 1966. This attractive row of shops and housing was a little past its best at the time the photograph was taken but is still highly pleasing overall.

Church Street and Tower Street in October 1966 with Scott the jeweller and Andrew Watt toys, tobacco and newsagents.

A splendid art nouveau window panel at the Tower Street shop of Stokells the decorators, 1966.

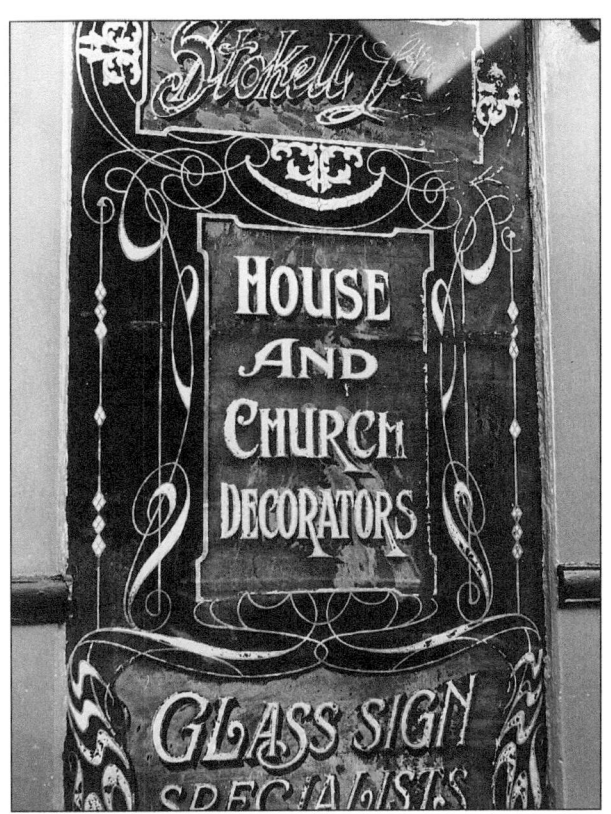

Stockton Street and Arthur Street awaiting demolition in 1966 prior to road widening improvements.

Stockton Street in October 1966. A well known and fondly remembered rendezvous was Masons Waverley cafe.

Stockton Street and Albion Street, October 1968. The college of further education can be seen under construction at the rear.

Church Street in October 1966 showing Alf Willings, nautical instrument makers and compass adjusters. Next door are P.J. Gjertson, ships chandlers and Edward Hudson, general printers.

Cliff Reynold's Central Garage, Whitby Street, October 1966. At the side of the building was where the Lex Cinema was situated.

Robinsons Liverpool House, Lynn Street, October 1966.

Northgate in December 1966. The Pools Dye Works shop is boarded up and next door is Blooms the pawnbrokers then Pools Surplus Stores, Walkers and the Globe Hotel. Blooms displays a cluster of three brass balls, the traditional pawnbroker's sign.

Hartlepool High Street, December 1966. The Fisherman's Arms is on the left, the former Workingmen's Club in the centre and F.W. Mason printers and stationer is on the right.

Southgate with the Heugh Social Club in the centre, January 1967.

Northgate, March 1967. Included are Blooms the pawnbroker, Pools Surplus Stores, A. Walker, the Globe Hotel and Walters general store. The pedestrian crossing leads to Cleveland Road.

Marks and Spencers together with Boots the Chemist and Stanton shoes at the corner of Lynn Street and Lambton Street in 1968.

Musgrave Street with Charles Dickens tool shop in the centre in 1968.

Lynn Street in 1968 with Hills the bakers, Sages Booksellers and Stationers and Radio Rentals.

Woolworths, Lynn Street, 1968.

The Market Buildings with the famous Lamb clock in Lynn Street, 1968. The shops include; Eagle, Scotch Wool shop, Singer, Find It Out, H. Lamb, and Delifare.

The wrought iron decorative gates of the Market entrance leading into the indoor hall which housed a wonderland of stalls and small shop units. One of the best remembered shops was Bretts the toffee and sweet maker whose aroma of toffee wafted throughout the hall and into the market yard. The Civic Restaurant (formerly the British Restaurant) was situated at the rear of the hall. It was later transferred to the new shopping centre and renamed the Windsor. The Scotch wool shop is also shown in this 1968 scene.

The corner of Lynn Street and Musgrave Street with Hardy & Co. furniture, the Ward Jackson Hotel and Robinsons, 1968.

Lynn Street with Marks and Spencer and Boots the Chemist, 1968. Note the dresses at 59s 6d.

Lynn Street, 1968. Weaver To Wearer sold suits to measure for £8 19s 6d and jackets for 79s 6d. Nearby were Workwear supplies and Maynards sweets. The main building is the Athenaeum which was built in 1851.

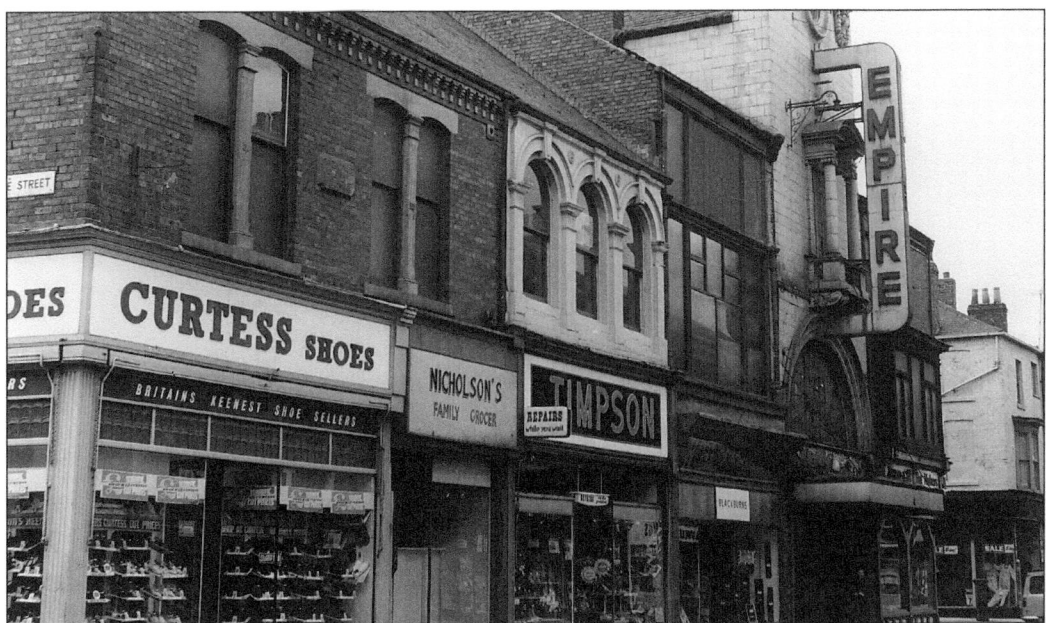

Lynn Street in 1968 with Curtess shoes, Timpsons shoes, Blackburns menswear, the Empire Theatre and Dunns the hatters. The West Hartlepool Empire Palace was opened in 1909 by Moss Empires, with a performance of *The Toreadors* by West Hartlepool Amateur Operatic Society (The WHODS). The first manager was Geo. F. Thompson and the conductor of the 20 strong orchestra was Edward Rogers. Seating for 2,000 people was provided and the building cost £20,000 at the time. After a successful and chequered history it was finally demolished in 1975.

Halfords motor and cycle accessories and Farm Stores, Lynn Street, 1968.

Lynn Street in 1968 showing Currys coffee house. Also in the photograph are W. Duncan the provision grocers, Delifare Ltd and H. Lamb jewellers and goldsmiths who had the renowned clock.

J.G. Clarke the chemist in Lynn Street at the corner of Hope Street in 1968. Hartlepool Photographic Society met regularly in the upstairs premises. Next door are Smart & Co. and Kents carpets and linos.

The Chain Lending Library, Lynn Street, 1968. For a small fee customers could borrow mainly fiction books. Next to this are John Temple the personal tailor, Tates radio supplies shop and the Direct Raincoat Ltd.

On the Lynn Street and Charles Street corner stood Burton tailors and the Market Hotel in 1968. Only the Market Hotel remains today.

Dovecot Salerooms were located in Lynn Street in 1968. They later moved into the premises of Blacketts in Church Street. Also shown is J.F. Lormor the newsagent and tobacconist.

Lynn Street at the corner of Lamb Street, with the main building of M. Robinson & Son Ltd department store on one side and Dovecot salerooms on the other.

The premises of Dunn & Co., hat maker and gentlemen's outfitters, next to the Empire Theatre and Timpsons shoes in Lynn Street, 1968.

At the Church Street end of Lynn Street the side of the Shades Hotel is visible and next to it are A. Walker the butcher, Beverly Photographic Studios, Pools Surplus Stores and City Stylish menswear.

The Durham Hotel and Paige ladies fashions at the corner of Exeter Street and Lynn Street in 1968.

John Blundells furniture store, Maurices ladies accessories and John Collier men's tailors ('The window to watch') at the junction of Lynn Street and Charles Street in 1968.

Graftons ladies fashions in Musgrave Street on the corner of Lynn Street, 1968.

Lynn Street in 1968 with Bannett-Hutton ladies fashion, Peter Pell men's clothiers and the North Eastern Hotel.

Shoefayre, Northern Furnishing Co. and Granthams, Lynn Street, 1968.

A. Hector Grabham the well known painters and decorators, 1968. Next to which are the Bamboo Chinese restaurant and Dalkins for men's shirts, ties and accessories.

Two of a number of house furnishers in Lynn Street in 1968 were Granthams and Northern Furnishers.

Lynn Street in 1968 showing Greenwoods the menswear shop, Saxone shoes and Woodhouse furnishers.

The Commercial Hotel next door to Books fashions and Easifit shoe shop, Lynn Street, 1968.

The popular Musgrave Street in 1968. The many shops include the Fruit Market, Moores provision stores, Hills the bakers, Atkinson and Shires pork butchers and J. Farrah the fishmongers.

Middlegate, May 1968. The premises shown are the shops of Robson the butcher and Davison the newsagent.

Blooms clothiers, jewellers and pawnbrokers, May 1968. The shop next door is Pools Surplus Stores.

Oxford Street, 1969. St Aidan's church hall is just behind the parked van. Former shops include the Co-op Chemists, Cullingfords general dealers, Gardners fishmonger, Colerossi ice cream, Rules Radio, Eclipse fruiterers, Pyles fish and chip shop, Handleys post office.

The popular lunch time venue, the Cosy Cafe, Scarborough Street, March 1969.

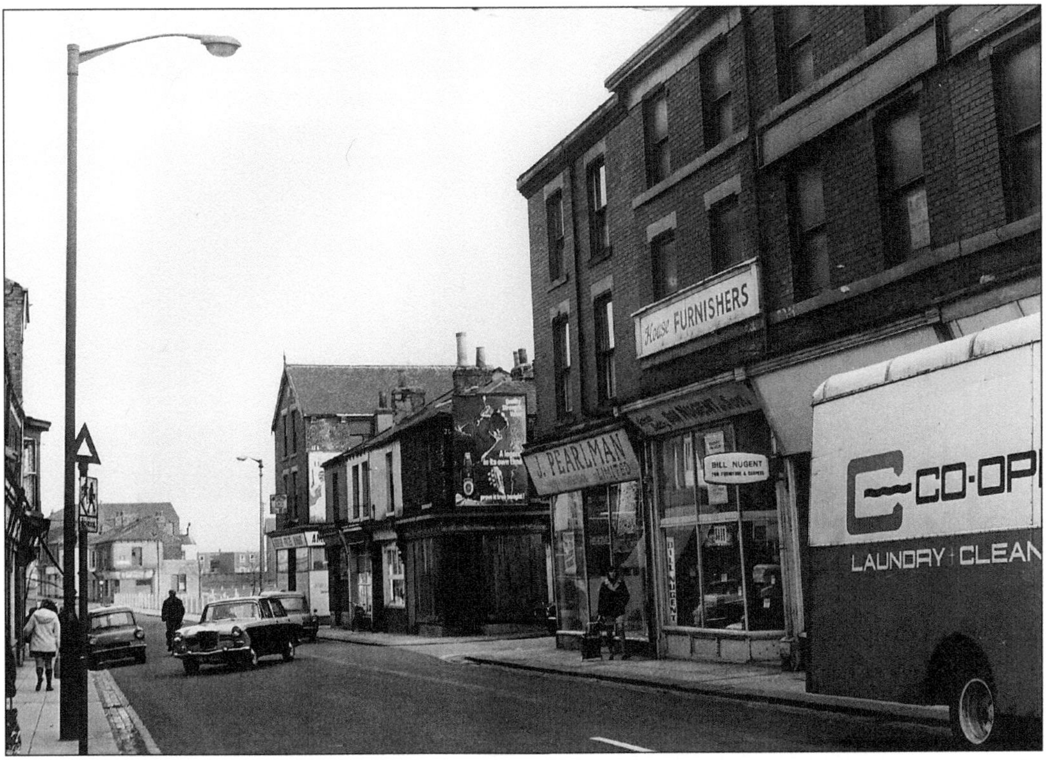
House FURNISHERS
J. PEARLMAN
BILL NUGENT
LAUNDRY

A 1971 view of Musgrave Street showing Bill Nugent carpets and furniture and the 'ticket club' shop of J. Pearlman (West Hartlepool) Ltd.

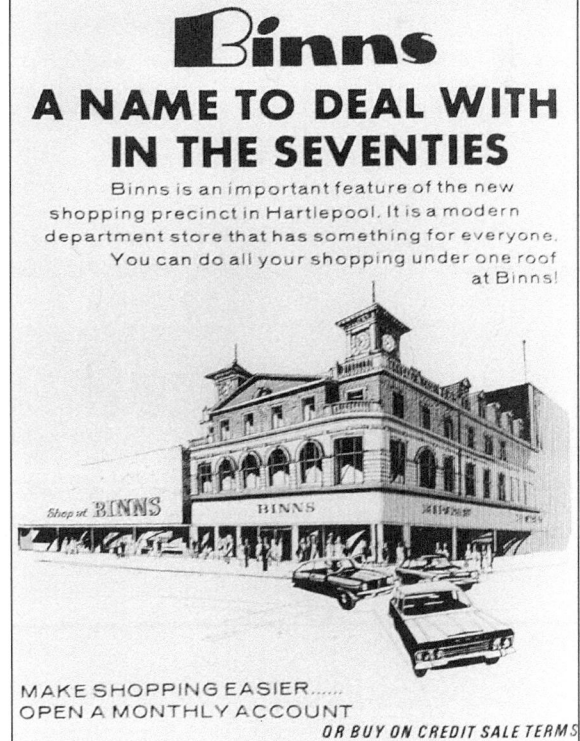

Binns
A NAME TO DEAL WITH IN THE SEVENTIES
Binns is an important feature of the new shopping precinct in Hartlepool. It is a modern department store that has something for everyone. You can do all your shopping under one roof at Binns!
Shop at BINNS
BINNS
MAKE SHOPPING EASIER......
OPEN A MONTHLY ACCOUNT
OR BUY ON CREDIT SALE TERMS

Binns department store as advertised in 1972.

The well known provision store of Liptons in York Road where red salmon was 20p a tin in 1973. Next door is Scorers Ltd ironmongers and hardware. St George's church is at the junction with Park Road.

The circular pedestrian ramp of the shopping centre was open to the elements in 1975.

The demolition of the Regent buildings at the corner of York Road and Park Road in 1976. The union jacks flying from the scaffolding were discovered in the loft and provided a defiant gesture. Next door was the Audi showroom of Jock Rae.

The popular department store of Blacketts at the corner of Church Street and Whitby Street in the early 1960s.

The Mail Clock at the Middleton Grange shopping centre, 1977.

One of the malls in the Middleton Grange shopping centre in 1972.

Four

The Call of the Sea

An aerial view of West Hartlepool in 1950 including the Old Town and Swainson Dock. The large buildings include the Nemco Match Factory, later to be destroyed by a spectacular fire in 1954. The town centre housing of the 'A' streets is in the foreground.

The spectacular blaze at the Match Factory at Swainson Dock on 30 August 1954 .

Discharging wood pulp and pit props at Union Dock, 1950.

A ship discharging wood pulp products for the paper industry, Hartlepool Docks, 1950.

The Heugh Lighthouse, Hartlepool Headland, 1951.

An aerial view of the Hartlepool and West Hartlepool dock areas in July 1963.

The Coal Dock and Staithes, 1961. The Central Marine Engine Works is in the background. Design students from the College of Art make sketches of the location.

A view of the docks from the C.M.E.W. crane in 1963. The ship is unloading timber products from Scandinavia. On the horizon can be seen the British Steel, North Works.

Hartlepools docklands with Wm Gray Shipyard, February 1964.

Coal being loaded into a ship at one of the Hartlepool Coal Staithes, 1964. The coal was gravity loaded and shipped mainly to the Thames for power stations in the South East.

An aerial view of Victoria Dock from the 1960s showing numerous buildings connected with the fishing industry. At the top left is the North Sea Oil Exploration Base. The Ice Making Factory is the large building, centre left. The old Hartlepool Railway Station in Northgate is partly visible in the foreground.

Victoria Terrace in March 1965. This building, later to be demolished, was originally built to house professional people and sea captains and in later years was used for ships supplies, butchers and chandlers.

Jackson and Union Docks in May 1965.

Medds Egg Warehouse, Victoria Terrace, October 1966. West Hartlepool was once the largest importer of eggs in the country.

The Coal Dock from the Staithes showing Harbour Terrace in 1966 where a number of engineering companies operated. In the background can be seen the Custom House and old Dock Office.

Swainson Dock with the offices of Wm Gray and the swing bridge across the channel, 1966.

The Custom House, Victoria Terrace, October 1966. The building was originally the Ship Inn pub and reputedly had the longest bar in England. The clock tower of the Dock Office is just visible.

Middleton Road with the swing bridge, Union Dock, October 1967. Timber imports are being stored on the quayside.

An aerial view of West Hartlepool Docks showing Swainson Dock in the foreground which is now filled in. Jackson Dock is in the centre and Union Dock at top of the picture. The site is presently occupied by the Historic Quay, Hartlepool Museum, Jackson's Landing Factory Shopping, Mecca Bingo, Old West Quay pub/hotel and Asda.

An aerial view of Hartlepool Dock in October 1967. The General Post Office is at the bottom left and Church Street is across the centre. Swainson Dock and the Wm Gray offices are at centre left. Union Dock, Coal Dock and Jackson Dock are prominent in the centre. Richardsons Westgarth Engine Works and the 'swan necked crane' are at the top right.

The offices of Wm Gray at Swainson Dock, just prior to demolition in June 1968.

Discharging sawn wood imported from Russia at the Union Dock, 1969.

A very active maritime scene at the Union Dock in 1972.

Five

Civic Events

The Council Chamber, Municipal Buildings, West Hartlepool, 1960. The Mayoral and Aldermanic chairs are raised above those of the councillors and officials. Later the council transferred to the present Civic Centre in Victoria Road and the old Grade II listed Municipal Buildings were completely refurbished as prestige office accommodation. The group painting on the wall depicts the first council meeting in 1887 and the painting on the right is a portrait of Ralph Ward Jackson, founder of West Hartlepool, the other being of George Pyeman.

Ald. R.W. Richardson JP, right, arriving at Buckingham Palace to receive the MBE for public service accompanied by Mrs O. Richardson JP and their son Ron Richardson.

The last council meeting of Hartlepool Council, 1967. Back row: left to right, Ald. Chambers, L.O. Williams (Town Clerk), Cllr D. Waller, Mayor, Ald. F. Jacques, Ald. F. Windebank. Front row: L. Davies (Deputy Borough Treasurer), T. Busby (Administration), S. Storm (Deputy Town Clerk), J.C. Haynes (Borough Engineer).

The final meeting of West Hartlepool Council held in the Town Hall, 20 March 1967. The Mayor at the time was Cllr George Groves JP.

The Mayor Cllr W.H. Iseley and the Mayoress Mrs B. Brotherton welcome girl guides from Sweden in 1969.

Princess Anne, escorted by the Mayor, Ald. Mrs A.I. Tuson, makes her way to the official opening of the Middleton Grange shopping centre, 27 May 1970.

Large crowds gather to watch as Princess Anne unveils the name plaque in the shopping centre, 27 May 1970.

The Mayor Ald. Mrs E. Sprintall and the Mayoress, Mrs M. Windale with the Duchess of Kent at the official opening of Hartlepool General Hospital, 16 June 1972.

The Mayor and Mayoress of Hartlepool, Cllr Ray and Mrs Jean Waller welcome members of the symphony orchestra of Battle Creek, Michigan, USA in Ward Jackson Park in 1975.

Post War Mayors

Hartlepool

1946-47	G. Davison
1948	T. Wood
1949	F. Jacques
1950-51	F. Windebank
1952	A.J. Orley
1953	W.C. Pounder
1954	D. Richmond
1955	R.S. Boswell
1956	T. Marine
1957	W.W. Emerson
1958	C. Chambers
1959	R.W. Richardson
1960	Mrs M.E. Smith
1961	T.T. Aird
1962	O.F. Bradshaw
1963	T.I. Boagey
1964	W. Glaister
1965	Mrs D. Charlton
1966	D. Waller

West Hartlepool

1946	H.H. Ryan
1947-48	T.W. Pinkney
1949	T.V. Oldfield
1950	B.H. Arnison
1951	H.L. Hogg MBE
1952-53	J.O.F. Hewlett OBE, TD,
	JP (resigned 8 Jan
1954)	
1953	R.Hand (15 Jan 1954)
1954	J.W. Miller
1955	C.E. Johnson BEM
1956	Mrs W Breward JP
1957	T. Breward
1958	J. Bratton JP
1959	T Andrews
1960	J.O. Coxen
1961	D.R. Ashton
1962	F.W. Crisp
1963	J. Addison
1964	Mrs B.E. Mann JP
1965	C.R. Warnes
1966	G.W. Groves JP

County Borough of Hartlepool

1967	F. Jacques JP
1968	W.H. Iseley
1969	G.P.K. Gallimore MA
1970	Mrs A.J. Tuson
1971	J.A. Pounder MBE, TD
1972	Mrs E. Sprintall
1973	W.O. Mann

District Council of Hartlepool

1974	K. McIntyre

Borough of Hartlepool

1974	R.Waller JP
1975	J. Bowers BEM
1976	J.C. Herbert
1977	J.W. Mason
1978	H.S. Gardener
1979	B. Hanson
1980	W. Middleton
1981	G.E. Ellett
1982	C. Stubbs
1983	J. Jones
1984	M. Lennon
1985	Mrs M. Boagey
1986	R. Barnfather BEM
1987	Mrs M. Watson
1988	J. Macrea
1989	Mrs M. Kellman
1990	J. Lynch
1991	T. Lloyd
1992	V. Burton
1993	B. Smith
1994	Mrs S.G. Hanson
1995	Mrs S.G. Worthy JP
1996	H.J. Bishop
1997	Mrs M. Doyle

Six

An Enterprising Place

The North Works of South Durham Iron & Steel Co., 1950. The timber (pit prop) yards are quite visible in the background.

An aerial view of the North Works in the late 1950s. Near the top right is the Expanded Metal Co. factory complex from which the Steelworks Bridge leads to Coronation Drive.

An aerial view of Seaton Carew North, c. 1950. At the centre right is Seaton swimming baths, later to be demolished. The Staincliffe Hotel is on the left at the front of the 'square' of buildings. Pit props destined for the Durham coal fields are stacked in the timber storage yard.

A meeting of the Hartlepools Advisory Committee, 16 May 1951, consisting of local dignitaries including George Groves, second from the right.

An aerial view of Hartlepool and the Headland from the 1960s with Steetley Magnesite Works prominent in the foreground.

A steam train passing under Newburn Bridge in 1964.

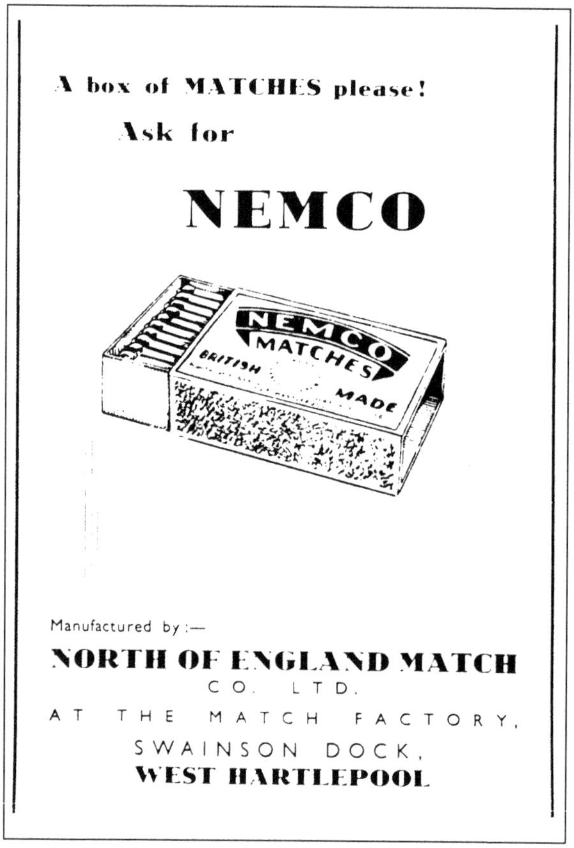

An advertisement for the North of England Match Co. (Nemco) from the early 1960s.

The grain driers of J.W. Cameron Brewers, November 1964.

Hartlepool (Old) Railway Station, Northgate, in a somewhat dilapidated condition in 1965 prior to demolition.

The interior of the old Railway Station in the 1960s. The platform and waiting rooms are clearly visible.

Powlett Road Gas Works in 1965. The works were later dismantled when natural gas was introduced. The site is now a private housing development.

South Durham Steel & Iron Co., South Works in the 1960s, construction of which started in 1958.

The Mill, Stranton Green, November 1966. Comet Electrical now stands on this site.

Middleton Road Gas Works offices and gasometer, November 1966.

The derelict Rope Works off West View Road in December 1967. Steel ropes were supplied to Durham coal miners and local engineering establishments.

The Seaton High Light in the grounds of Batchelor Robinson, Longhill, 1967. The Light was re-erected stone by stone at Jackson's Landing by the Teesside Development Corporation.

J.J. Hardy & Sons, Brass Foundry at the corner of Old Cemetery Road, November 1967.

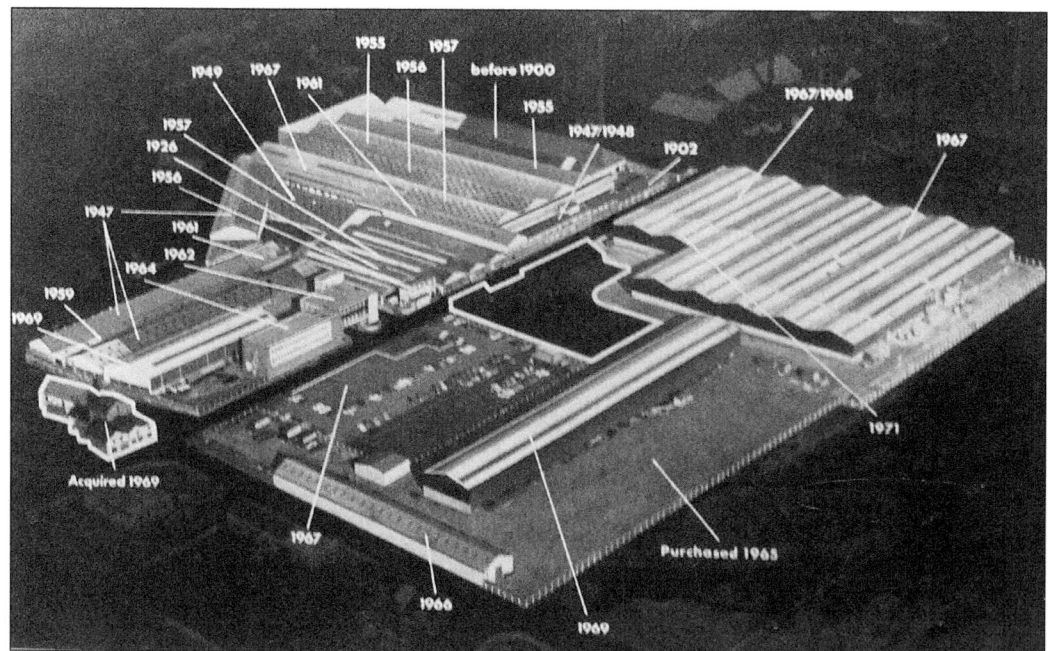

The factory in Brenda Road of Aladdin Industries, 1969. The company were manufacturers of vacuum flasks for export and home use. The building was later converted to car showrooms and workshops by Parsons of Hartlepool and then a Health and Fitness Centre.

The site plan of the Expanded Metal Co. in 1972. At the time they were the world's largest exporter of expanded metal.

An aerial view of the Steel
Works slag tip during
clearance of the North
Works. Tees Bay Retail
Park now occupies the site.

British Steel Corporation's
150 inch plate mill at
the South Works near
Greatham, 1970. The
plant was one of the finest
in Europe and is now no
more.

the
long
view

A 1970 brochure advertisement for the building of Hartlepool Nuclear Power Station, Tees Road.

Hartlepool Nuclear Power Station, Tees Road, 1987.

Seven

At Leisure

Floodlit tulip beds in Ward Jackson Park, 1946.

The Annual outing from the Blacksmith Arms, Stranton, c. 1950.

The bathing pool on the Headland in its heyday. The pool was largely destroyed during the great storm of 1953.

The Block Sands and paddling pool, 1950. This was a popular venue during the summer for families and young children.

A toy jeep provides enjoyment in Burbank Street. Peter Brown is on left and Michael Hadfield, right.

This may be the
lucky programme   N⁰ 4337

WEST HARTLEPOOL GARDENS GUILD
(Member of West Hartlepool Council of Social Service)

Programme

Coronation Year

SHOW & EXHIBITION

WARD JACKSON PARK
WEST HARTLEPOOL

Saturday, 15th August, 1953 from 12 noon to 9 p.m.

Official opening at 1 p.m. by
HIS WORSHIP THE MAYOR OF WEST HARTLEPOOL,
(Coun. J. O. F. HEWLETT, O.B.E., T.D., J.P.)

Admission by this programme 2/-

Children, with parents — 1/- (pay at gate)
Old Age Pensioners producing Pension Book — 1/- (pay at gate)

The summer programme for the Coronation Year Show and Exhibition, Ward Jackson Park,
August 1953.

A happy country scene with haymaking on the farm where the Red Admiral Hotel now stands.

The Empire Theatre, Lynn Street in 1968.

The Empire Theatre Auditorium, 1951.

The Empire Theatre, West Hartlepool in 1951 showing the very fine Crush Room in all its glory.

The Empire Theatre Orchestra with their leader Bert Hewitt, 1949.

A celebrity concert held in the Empire Theatre, Lynn Street in July 1951 in aid of the Easington Pit disaster fund. Left to right: Harry Metcalf (theatre manager), Tommy Trinder ('you lucky people'), Jack Radcliffe and Norman Evans ('over the garden wall').

George Armitage conducts the Geo. Armitage Singers during rehearsals for their only performance of *Samson*, c. 1960.

The Ward Jackson Hotel, Lynn Street, October 1968.

The extremely pleasant conservatory situated within the Gray Art Gallery and Museum, Clarence Road in the 1960s. The fine marble statues survive to this day although not on public display.

Surtees Street with the Atlantic Hotel and a Reliant Robin, October 1966.

The Engineers' club in Raby Road, October 1966. It was a popular and well situated venue for boxing tournaments.

The North Eastern Hotel, Lynn Street, 1966.

The Queens Cinema (the Old Town Hall), Lumley Street, 1966. The building was later damaged by fire and demolished.

The crowded Fish Sands on the Headland during the height of summer in 1966.

The Palladium (formerly the Theatre Royal and The Empress) in Northgate, March 1967. Pat's prize bingo is an indication of the changing times.

The North Eastern Hotel, Lynn Street 1968. Next door is 'Dress Well with Peter Pell'.

The Market Hotel, Lynn Street, 1968.

The Star Hotel, Lynn Street, 1968.

Hartlepool Church Choral Union Third Annual Dinner, 1968. Left to right: Gwen Kidd, Harry Pickard, Lucy Gibson, Lilian Hare, Alec Telfer, Eveline Smith, Candish Chisholm, Stanley Smith (secretary), Gladys Arrowsmith, Marjorie D. Richardson (musical director).

West Hartlepool Rugby Football Club, 1st XV, winners of the Durham Senior Cup, 1970-71.

The official opening of West Hartlepool Rugby Football Club's new clubhouse in 1970. Left to right: R. Turner (Chairman WHRFC), W.C. Ramsay CBE (President Rugby Football Union), T. Metcalfe (President WHRFC).

Mr Ron Grubb, Director of Parks, with members of his delighted staff after Hartlepool won the Britain in Bloom Cities Trophy for the fourth consecutive year in 1972. Hartlepool was the overall regional winner and subsequently shared the Great Britain City trophy with Bath.

Eight

Towards the
Twenty-first Century

The refurbished Old Municipal Buildings in Church Square, 1997.

Christ Church Art Gallery and on the left the Old Municipal Buildings which are now prestigious offices in Church Square.

A view from Upper Church Street with the Wesley chapel, the Town Hall Theatre, the Mail Office and Benefits Agency and Council offices which were originally the old police station on the right.

118

The Central Library in York Road was purpose built of modern design occupying the site of the former Northern's Cinema.

Where Longscar Hall stood in Seaton Carew is now an up to date pub/wine bar and leisure complex.

Tees Bay Retail Park off Brenda Road. This development was built on the site of the former North steelworks slag bank from where the term 'Wagga Moon' originated.

Hartlepool Marina looking across what once was the Coal Dock. At the rear is the Custom House (Ship Inn), the Dock Office and the Old West Quay public house/motel.

Jackson's Dock from the Coal Dock showing Jackson's Landing shopping complex. The relocated Seaton High Light is at the extreme right.

The Lock Gates and Control House of Hartlepool Marina looking west. Seaton High Light is clearly visible.

The New housing development at the Marina off Chandlers Walk. The Headland is visible in the background.

A view of the recently reconstructed West Harbour/South Docks area where the original 'Skeleton Pier' once stood.

The Old West Quay motel and pub stands on the site of once busy dock activities.

The restored SS *Wingfield Castle*, which was built and commissioned in West Hartlepool, moored off the quayside of the Museum of Hartlepool with the majestic masts of HMS *Trincomalee* located within the Historic Quay.

The Hartlepool Council owned, Museum of Hartlepool and Quayside has proved to be a popular and record breaking museum.

Part of the Mecca Bingo and leisure complex in the Marina area.

An exterior view of Hartlepool Historic Quay. It is a unique 'museum' experience of considerable interest and importance using the latest presentation technology.

The new road system through the Marina with Asda superstore and in the background, Victoria Park, Hartlepool United Football ground.

The restored Church Street with the relocated statue of Ralph Ward Jackson, the founder of West Hartlepool, looking east towards the sea.

The redesigned Victory Square and War Memorial with its impressive lighting arrangement. The Civic Centre and Law Courts overlook the scene.

Hartlepool College of Education, Stockton Street showing the extensions with the bistro and beauty/hairdressing salon at the front.

Tesco superstore off Belle Vue Way. A popular store with traditional yet up to date design features.

Much of the town property has been considerably improved in recent years as these Derwent Street houses show.

The light and spacious Central Square of Middleton Grange shopping centre after modernisation.